FOOTPATHS OF
SCOTLAND

LOMOND

This edition published by
LOMOND BOOKS 2003

Published by
Parragon
Queen Street House
4 Queen Street
Bath BA1 1HE

Created and produced by
The Bridgewater Book Company Ltd,
Lewes, East Sussex

ISBN 1-84204-063-4

Printed in China

www.walkingworld.com

Visit the Walkingworld website at
www.walkingworld.com

All the walks in this book are available in more
detailed form on the Walkingworld website.
The route instructions have photographs at key
decision points to help you to navigate, and
each walk comes with an Ordnance Survey®
map. Simply print them out on A4 paper
and you are ready to go! A modest annual
subscription gives you access to over 1,400
walks, all in this easy-to-follow format. If you
wish, you can purchase individual walks for a
small fee.

Next to every walk in this book you will see
a Walk ID. You can enter this ID number on
Walkingworld's 'Find a Walk' page and you will
be taken straight to the details of that walk.

CONTENTS

Introduction

Scotland is a fabulous place to walk. It is blessed with a varied and beautiful landscape, a dense network of public footpaths and places of historical interest at every corner. Add to all this the many thousands of well-placed pubs, tea shops and visitor attractions, and it's easy to see why walking is a treasured pastime for millions of people.

Walking is the perfect way to keep fit and healthy. It is good for your heart, muscles and body generally, without making the extreme demands of many sports. For most walkers, however, the health benefits are secondary. We walk for the sheer pleasure of it — being able to breathe in the fresh air, enjoy the company of our friends and 'get away from it all'.

Equipment

If you take up walking as a hobby, it is quite possible to spend a fortune on specialist outdoor kit. But you really don't need to. Just invest in a few inexpensive basics and you'll be ready to enjoy any of the walks in this book.

For footwear, boots are definitely best as they provide you with ankle support and protection from the inevitable mud, nettles and puddles. A lightweight pair should be fine if you have no intention of venturing up big hills or over rugged terrain. If you are not sure what to get, go to a specialist shop and ask for advice. Above all, choose boots that fit well and are comfortable.

Take clothing to deal with any weather that you may encounter. Allow for the 'wind-chill' factor – if your clothes get wet you will feel this cooling effect even more. Carry a small rucksack with a spare top, a hat and waterproofs, just in case. The key is being able to put on and take off layers of clothing at will and so keep an even, comfortable temperature throughout the day.

It's a good idea to carry some food and drink. Walking is exercise and you need to replace the fluid you lose through perspiration. Take a bottle of soft drink or water, and sip it regularly rather than downing it in one go. The occasional chocolate bar, sandwich or biscuit can work wonders when energy levels are flagging.

Walking poles – the modern version of the walking stick – are worth considering. They help you to balance and allow your arms to take some of the strain when going uphill. They also lessen the impact on your knees on downhill slopes. Don't be fooled into thinking that poles are just for the older walker – they are popular with trekkers and mountaineers of all ages.

Finding your way

Most walkers use Ordnance Survey® maps, rightly considered to be among the most accurate, up-to-date and 'walker-friendly' in the world. The 1:50,000 scale Landranger series has long been a favourite of outdoor enthusiasts. Almost all areas of Britain are also covered by the more detailed 1:25,000 scale Explorer and Explorer OL series. These include features such as field boundaries, farm buildings and small streams.

Having a map and compass – and learning how to use them – is vital to being safe in the countryside. Compass and map skills come with practice – there is no substitute for taking them out and having a go. Buy a compass with a transparent base plate and rotating dial; you will find this type in any outdoor shop. Most come with simple instructions – if not, ask in the shop for a guide.

If this all sounds a bit serious, I urge you not to worry too much about getting lost. We have all done it – some of us more often than we care to admit! You are unlikely to come to much harm unless you are on a featureless hilltop or out in very poor weather. If you want to build up your confidence, start with shorter routes through farmland or along the coastline and allow yourself plenty of time.

key to maps

✆	Telephone	☖	Lighthouse
❶	Start of walk		Camping
	Viewpoint	▲	Youth hostel
Δ	Pylon		Bridge
	Triangulation point		Windmill
☖	Mast		Highest point/summit
⛪	Church with Steeple	PH	Public house
	Church without Steeple	PC	Public convenience
⛪	Chapel	1666	Place of historical interest
	Power		Embankment/cutting
⚑	Golf course		Rocky area/ sharp drop
	Picnic area		Building
	Car park		Castle
	Information	☆	Tumulus
			Garden

There are plenty of walks in this book that are perfect for the beginner. You can make navigating even easier by downloading the routes in this book from Walkingworld's website: www.walkingworld.com. These detailed walk instructions feature a photograph at each major decision point, to help you confirm your position and see where to go next.

Another alternative is to join a local walking group

⸜⸝⸌	Marsh	Lake/sea
⸱⬤⸱	Railway station	
	Dismantled railway	Woods
▪ ▪ ▪ ▪ ▪	Route of walk	
▬▬▬	A Road	Sand
▬▬▬	B Road	Dunes
	Footpath	Urban
	Track/unclassified road	
	Stream	
	River	
	Large river	

0   1 km   1 mile

Difficulty Rating

Gentle Stroll   Moderate Walk

Easy Walk   Hill Scramble

Time

⬤ Each circle = 1 hour

◗ Half circle = ½ hour

and learn from others. There are hundreds of such groups around the country, with members keen to share their experience and skills.

Enough words. Take the walks in this book as your inspiration. Grab your map and compass, and put on your boots. It's time to go out and walk!

Have fun.

DAVID STEWART *Walkingworld*

▲ Map: Explorer 309
▲ Distance: 9 km/5¼ miles
▲ Walk ID: 824 Tony Brotherton

Difficulty rating

!!!

Time

●●●◗

▲ Hills or Fells, Sea, Pub, Toilets, Church, Castle, Wildlife, Birds, Flowers, Great Views, Butterflies, Food Shop

Dunskey Castle from Portpatrick

```
                    Stranraer   A75
Portpatrick  ◯  A77
                A716
```

From the port of Portpatrick this scenic walk heads south over the moorland by road, passing by the ruin of Dunskey Castle with its dramatic clifftop setting. The splendid coastal scenery, birds and flowers make this a walk to remember.

❶ From the car park pass by the old lighthouse and walk round the harbour as far as Main Street. Turn into Main Street, then into School Brae. Follow the road uphill and across the old railway bridge to the junction with the Old Military Road.

❷ Follow this road. It rises clear of Portpatrick and meets a junction. Keeping on the road, turn right across the moors, to reach the old railway viaduct.

❸ Continue along this moorland road. At the stone wall, pause to view Dunskey Castle in the distance. The road switchbacks on, past a joining road at North Port O'Spittal, then drops and bends sharply before the turn-off to Knockinaam Lodge Hotel. Turn right down the lane towards the hotel.

❹ At the top of the hotel car park, a sign points the way to Portpatrick via a cliff walk. The path climbs to the right. At the top cross two fields, exiting via the gate at the top corner of the second field. The curving path to the left leads down to Morroch Bay.

❺ Follow the path along the top of the cliffs, crossing occasional stiles. Look out for abundant birdlife on rocks and cliff-ledges. Dunskey Castle comes into view again and the path descends to a bridge over the burn. Cross the bridge and ascend the steps. The path meanders over the headland to Castle Bay.

❻ Follow the path round the top of the bay to Dunskey Castle. The path continues along the cliff top, with the old railway cutting below to the right. Portpatrick Hotel comes into sight. Follow the steps down to Portpatrick harbour. To return to the car park, retrace your steps by the old lighthouse.

One of the great joys of walking a route such as this one is the moment when a beautiful view opens out before you.

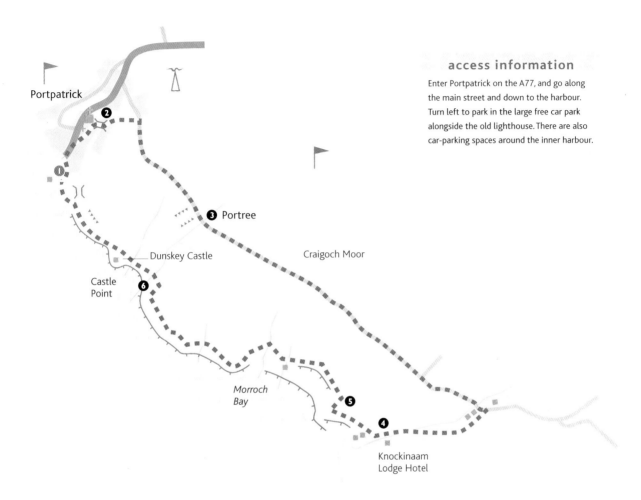

Portpatrick

①

②

③ Portree

Dunskey Castle

Castle
Point

⑥

Craigoch Moor

*Morroch
Bay*

⑤

④

Knockinaam
Lodge Hotel

access information

Enter Portpatrick on the A77, and go along
the main street and down to the harbour.
Turn left to park in the large free car park
alongside the old lighthouse. There are also
car-parking spaces around the inner harbour.

*The ruins of Dunskey Castle stand
out as a clear landmark at the top
of the cliff.*

further information

Look out for fulmars, kittiwakes, guillemots
and peregrine falcons around the cliffs above
Morroch Bay. Unusual wild flowers, including
spring squill and orchids, grow among the
more common thrift and campion.

0		1 km		1 mile

▲ Map: Explorer 330
▲ Distance: 11 km/6¾ miles
▲ Walk ID: 301 Simon Tweedie

Difficulty rating

Time

⬤ ⬤ ⬤ ⬤

▲ Hills or Fells, Mountains, River, Lake/Loch, National Trust/NTS, Wildlife, Birds, Flowers, Great Views

White Coomb from Grey Mare's Tail

This outstanding walk takes you to one of Scotland's highest waterfalls (known as the Grey Mare's Tail), a hidden glen and Loch Skeen. Listen out for the high-pitched call of the peregrine falcons which nest on the craigs.

❶ Leave by the steps on the north side of the car park. The path is steep and rises quickly to reveal spectacular views.

❷ When you reach the top of the falls, the glen above opens out. The path meanders, following the gentle flow of the burn. White Coomb looms high to the left with Lochcraig Head to the north. Continue on upwards until Loch Skeen comes into view to the left of the path.

❸ The route follows the eastern shore of the loch with no discernible path. Leaving the loch behind, the ground rises steeply. Follow a route to the east of the cliffs and up the steep grassy slope to the cairn at the top of Lochcraig Head. Follow the dry stone dyke left towards White Coomb.

❹ At Firthybrig Head the dyke takes a sharp left to a southerly direction. Follow this through Donald's Cleuch Head to Firthhope Rig. Here the dyke takes a sharp left. Follow the dyke a short way until it bears left. This is the closest landmark to the summit cairn, which lies about 100 paces to the south west.

❺ Return to the dyke from the summit and follow it down the hill until you reach Rough Craigs. Scramble down to the left of the dyke until you pick it up again at the bottom. Follow the dyke over Upper Tarnberry and down to meet the Tail Burn.

❻ The dyke ends on the Tail Burn where you cross. Pick up the Tail Burn path again on the other side and follow it back down to the car park.

A fabulous view of the Grey Mare's Tail waterfall from the opposite side of Tail Burn.

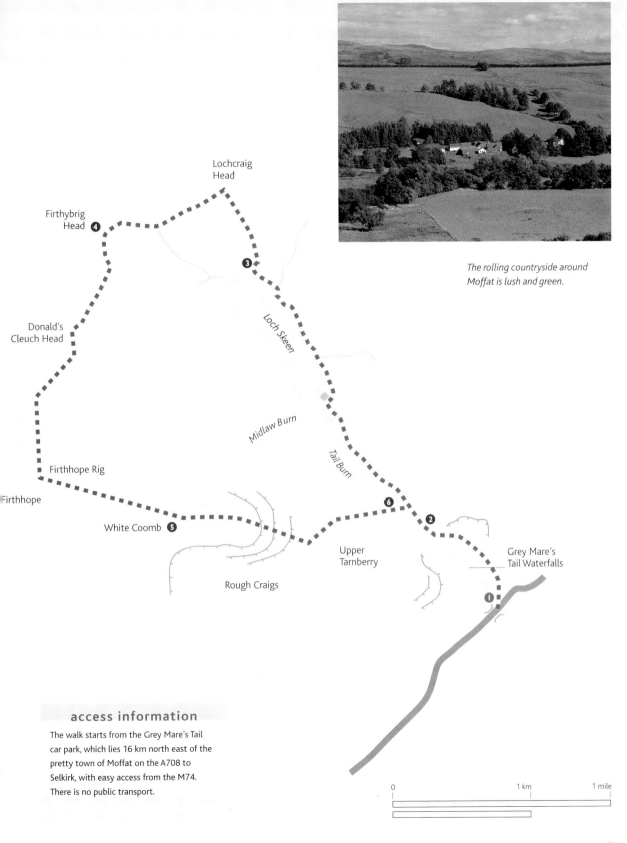

Lochcraig
Head

Firthybrig
Head ❹

❸

Donald's
Cleuch Head

Loch Skeen

Midlaw Burn

Tail Burn

Firthhope Rig

Firthhope

White Coomb ❺

❻

❷

Upper
Tarnberry

Grey Mare's
Tail Waterfalls

❶

Rough Craigs

The rolling countryside around
Moffat is lush and green.

access information

The walk starts from the Grey Mare's Tail
car park, which lies 16 km north east of the
pretty town of Moffat on the A708 to
Selkirk, with easy access from the M74.
There is no public transport.

0   1 km   1 mile

▲ Map: Explorer 326
▲ Distance: 6 km/3¾ miles
▲ Walk ID: 799 J. & D. Howat

Difficulty rating

🥾🥾

Time

⚫⚫

▲ Sea, Pub, Toilets, Museum, Play Area, Castle, National Trust/NTS Property, Wildlife, Birds, Flowers, Great Views

Maidens from Croy Bay

A linear coastal walk from Croy Bay through Culzean Country Park to reach Maidens, taking in part of the rugged headland by Culzean Castle. On a good day there are magnificent views towards Arran and the Mull of Kintyre.

❶ Leave the top car park and follow the road down to the lower car park at Croy Shore. Turn left on to the beach to reach some small cottages. Continue the walk in woodland parallel to the shore.

❷ At the next bay take the path away from the shore, past the Gas House and Gas Keeper's Cottage. Enter Culzean Park and follow the path up through the trees towards the castle.

❸ Branch left towards the castle's forecourt. Take the gate to the left of the castle, and follow the path along the side. Descend the steps to the gardens and Fountain Court. Continue south through the gardens, through a gap in the wall, into a grassy field. Cut across the field towards the sea. Follow the steps and go past the cannons to the boathouse beach and Dolphin House.

❹ Turn left, and continue carefully south along the rocky coast to the next bay. Take the steps and wooden walkway through a marshy area back to a T-junction on a well-trodden path.

❺ Turn right, and follow the path. Turn right again at the 'Cliff Walk' sign. The path eventually turns inland and descends to the Swan Pond. Turn to the right at the side of the pond, and walk a few metres to reach a junction with a smaller path off to the right.

❻ Leave the main path for a smaller one signposted to Port Carrick, Barwhin Hill. When you reach the edge of the park, fork left leading down to the beach at Maidens shore. Turn left and continue along the beach to reach the Maidens car park and the Bruce Hotel.

further information

The walk can easily be altered to become a circular walk if this is preferred. Once you reach the Swan Pond in Culzean Country Park, take any of the paths signposted towards the Home Farm, then return along the coast.

Watch out for the rocks and rising tides while you are walking along the shore beyond the castle.

access information

Take the A719 south from Ayr. Soon after
Croy Brae take the road to the right to Croy
Beach. Park either at the top or bottom of
the hill. As this is a linear walk, you will have
to retrace your steps unless you have a
companion prepared to meet you at the end
of the walk. To drive to the finishing car park,
continue south on the A719. Turn right at
the T-junction (towards Culzean Country
Park). Continue past the park entrance to
reach Maidens. At a sharp bend in the road
to the left, take the small road to the right.
Car parking is along this road.

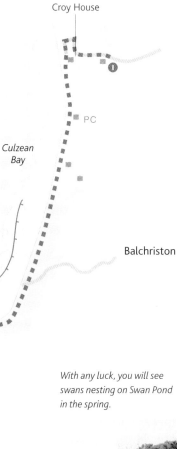

Croy House

PC

Culzean Bay

Balchriston

Culzean Castle

Culzean Country Park

*With any luck, you will see
swans nesting on Swan Pond
in the spring.*

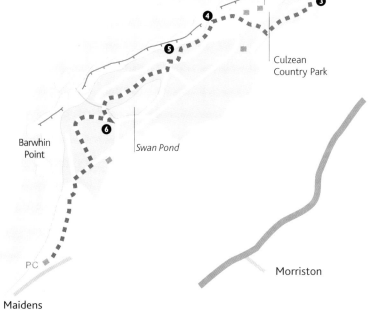

Barwhin Point

Swan Pond

Morriston

PC

Maidens

0   1 km   1 mile

▲ Map: Explorer 326
▲ Distance: 12 km/7½ miles
▲ Walk ID: 759 Jude Howat

Difficulty rating

👣

Time

●●●●

▲ Sea, Castle, Wildlife, Birds, Flowers, Great Views, Good for Kids, Public Transport

Heads of Ayr from Seafield

A beach walk, to be undertaken at low tide, taking you from central Ayr along the seafront, eventually reaching the magnificent cliffs known as the Heads of Ayr, returning via the old railway line.

1 Follow the promenade along the coast and cross the footbridge at the River Doon. Walk down on to the shore past the ruins of Greenan Castle and on to Deil's Dyke. Continue along the coast, passing a caravan park to walk under the Heads of Ayr. Continue along the shore. The path is just before the waterfalls on the next set of cliffs.

2 Follow the path from the shore up the hill, taking in the glorious views up the Firth of Clyde. At the top of the hill the path widens to a track.

3 Turn left on to the track, into a caravan park. At the first crossroads turn left, then immediately right. Walk the length of the park along the route of the old railway embankment. At the far end of the site exit via a gate. Carry straight on through the next, rusty gate. It may be overgrown, but passable. The route leads between two sets of fields. Climb the fence and continue to reach a rough track off to the right.

4 Turn right on to the rough track to reach the main road. Turn left and walk along the road past the paths leading to Farm Park and the Holiday Village. Exit back towards Ayr. Follow the National Cycle Route sign off to the left.

5 When the road bends sharply right, continue straight ahead through a field back down to the shore.

6 Turn right and walk back towards Greenan Castle, then retrace your steps to the start of the walk.

The ruins of Greenan Castle are perched on the cliff edge.

further information

Deil's Dyke is the name given to the rocks that are visible at low tide. IMPORTANT: Check the tides prior to starting the walk, as many of the headlands become impassable at high tide. **Tides**: http://www.uk.digiserve.com/ukfr/gbtide.htm Select Ayr for tide times.

access information

Free parking is available at the seafront just next to the Seafield roundabout. Ayr is also very well served by both buses and trains – follow signs towards the shore from either station to reach the start of the walk. The walk can be made shorter by parking at Doonfoot and starting at the footbridge over the River Doon.

Difficulty rating

Time

▲ Sea, Wildlife, Birds, Flowers, Great Views, Moor

Birsay to Marwick

Amazing cliff views.

This linear walk traverses the top of the cliffs of the west coast of Orkney. This coast possibly has the best sea cliffs on Orkney and there are excellent views. Of particular interest are the seabird colonies on the cliffs, which include puffins, guillemots and fulmars.

❶ Approaching from the B9056, start by following the track that heads straight on between the field gate and a standing stone that forms the corner of a fence. (This is the track heading due west from the corner, not the one heading north.) After 300 m and an open area (sometimes used for parking) the track bends to the left and starts to follow the coast. From the bend in the track there are good views back over the bay to the Brough of Birsay.

❷ Continue parallel to the cliff edge, now rising gently, along the path which is fairly indistinct at times. As you continue to climb, the cliffs to your side become larger.

❸ After about a kilometre of going gently uphill, a path comes in from the left (this is the direct route to the headland from a car park). This path becomes much more distinct, running between a fence and the cliff. There are excellent views back along the cliffs.

❹ When you reach the highest point, topped by the Kitchener Memorial, there are superb views south to the island of Hoy. The famous Old Man of Hoy is visible to the right of the cliffs. You can also see beyond to the Scottish mainland.

❺ A path continues past the memorial to rejoin the fence and then follows the fence to the south west before turning the headland and dropping downhill to the bay of Mar Wick.

❻ At the foot of the slope the path follows the water's edge to reach the road and the end of the walk.

further information

If transport cannot be arranged, an alternative to the end of the walk is to turn back from the memorial and retrace your steps to the gate. Go through the gate and follow a path to a car park from where you can follow the minor road back to your start point. This gives a total distance of 7 km for the walk.

access information

The route as described starts from the sharp left-hand bend on the B9056, where it overlooks Birsay Bay, and finishes on the shores of Mar Wick – another bay to the south of Marwick Head.

▲ Map: Explorer 11
▲ Distance: 17 km/10½ miles
▲ Walk ID: 171 Oliver O'Brien

Difficulty rating

Time

▲ Hills or Fells, River, Lake/Loch, Pub, Toilets, Great Views, Public Transport

Loch Ard Forest from Aberfoyle

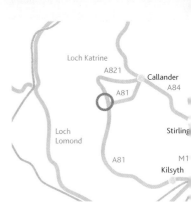

This long but easy walk, entirely on forest roads, tours Loch Ard Forest. The route includes a view of Loch Ard, an impressive Victorian aqueduct and superb views west to Ben Lomond.

1 Turn left out of the Visitor Centre and take the B829 west out of Aberfoyle.
2 At the restored mill, in Milton, turn left off the main road, cross a bridge and follow the road around, bearing right at the green Forest Enterprise signpost. Take the track to the right, past several houses. Cross a couple of gates, and continue along the track beside the loch shore. Bear right at the junction. Eventually Loch Ard opens out on the right. Here, the track meets the loch on the right again. Turn left at the junction and follow the track around to the left, climbing into the forest.
3 At the junction turn sharp right and continue to climb. After 200 m another track on the left joins this track. Bear right and follow the main forest track through the woodlands. Follow the main track, which starts to descend.
4 At the crossroads take a less distinct track to the left which swings back to the right and crosses under the aqueduct. Follow the track around beside electricity pylons, eventually passing another part of the aqueduct. The track passes under again before swinging back out. Continue along the track and follow the line of the aqueduct directly down the hill.

5 Cross Duchray Water on the bridge; there are stiles by both of its gates. Continue up the hill. Turn left and walk along the wide forest road, which crosses the Castle Burn three times.
6 Watch out for paths to your left that offer a pretty detour to Lochlan Spling. Otherwise, continue along the main forest track, which eventually turns into a road, passing several houses and a hotel. Turn left and follow the road, crossing over a narrow bridge and back into the centre of Aberfoyle.

access information

Aberfoyle can be reached from Glasgow by travelling north on Maryhill Road and the A81. If you are coming from the east or north, travel to Callander on the A84(T), then take the A81 west to Aberfoyle. Aberfoyle is one kilometre off the A81, on the A821. There is parking in the square at Aberfoyle, by the Tourist Information Centre. First Edinburgh operates a regular bus service (Nos. 10/11/C11) from Glasgow to/from Stirling via Balfron and Aberfoyle.

further information

Loch Ard Forest is a working forest managed by Forest Enterprise, and some forest tracks may be closed. Be aware that areas which were forested at the time of writing may have been cleared.

The track passes under this impressive section of the Victorian aqueduct running from Loch Katrine to Glasgow.

Loch Ard

Couligartan

Innis Ard

Duchray Castle

Duchray Water

Castle Burn

Milton

Dalzell Wood

Lochan Spling

Kirkton

B829

Visitor Centre Aberfoyle

0   1 km   1 mile

The outstanding features of this walk are the beautiful woodland setting and the waterside views.

▲ Map: Landranger 1
▲ Distance: 7 km/4³/₄ miles
▲ Walk ID: 1508 C. & J. Simpson

Difficulty rating

Time

▲ Features Sea, Birds, Flowers, Great Views, Moor, Nature Trail

Herma Ness

This walk is a superb mix of moorland and coastal walking to the cliffs of Herma Ness with its fine arches and array of offshore sea stacks. The return over Hermaness Hill gives good views over Muckle Flugga and its lighthouse.

❶ From the car park, pass through the gate, uphill a few metres and through another gate to follow the path which traverses the hillside, rising gently as you go. In time this leads to and then follows the burn of Winnaswarta Dale.

❷ Shortly after you start following the burn you come to a fork and a marker post. Take the left-hand fork. (The return route comes in on the path on the right). There follows a gradually rising section across open moor, with occasional stretches of boardwalk to protect sensitive areas of bog.

❸ At the marker post the view along the cliffs is spectacular, with thousands of seabirds. The route turns right and follows the cliffs, dipping slightly before rising again.

❹ As you start to rise again the views over to the rock arch, the stacks and Muckle Flugga lighthouse open out.

❺ For the return journey, marker posts leading off to the right take you up a well-worn path to the top of Hermaness Hill. The top of the hill has some lochans (small lakes) and more boardwalk sections. There are good views from the top of the hill although, in contrast to the wilderness on this side of the Burra Firth, Saxa Vord, the hill on the other side, is topped by a prominent early warning station. The descent over more boggy ground with numerous lochans is marked by a series of posts leading back to the junction.

❻ Rejoin the outward route further down the burn. Go back along the path to the car park.

The jagged rocks off the coast of Herma Ness are the northernmost point of Britain, and home to thousands of seabirds.

access information

The island of Unst is reached by two ferries from the Shetland mainland, including a drive over the island of Yell in between. On Unst follow the main road through Baltasound towards Haroldswick. Take the unclassified road on your left as you approach Haroldswick – signposted to Herma Ness and Burrafirth.

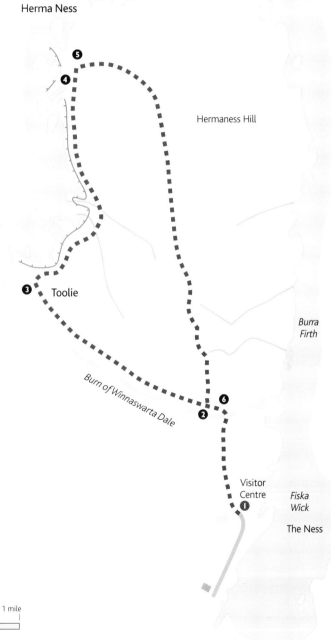

The Gord

Herma Ness

Hermaness Hill

further information

In season, the walk along the clifftops is made even more interesting by the thousands of puffins and other seabirds. You can watch gannets fishing offshore or just sitting in the great colonies at Herma Ness itself. (Take your binoculars.)

❺

❹

❸ Toolie

Burn of Winnaswarta Dale

Burra Firth

❻

❷

Visitor Centre

❶

Fiska Wick

The Ness

0   1 km   1 mile

▲ Map: Explorer 396
▲ Distance: 7 km/4³/₄ miles
▲ Walk ID: 864 Ian Cordiner

Difficulty rating

Time

▲ Sea, Pub, Toilets, Museum, Castle, Great Views, Food Shop, Public Transport, Nature Trail, Woodland, Ancient Monument

Dunnottar Castle from Stonehaven

A short walk through Stonehaven and on to the ruins of historic Dunnottar Castle, situated on dramatic sea cliffs. The walk returns to the scenic harbour area of the town and finally to the market square via a boardwalk by the seashore.

❶ Leave the square in the town centre by going south along Barclay Street. At the end turn right. Cross to the other side of the street then go over the pedestrian bridge. Immediately take the path to the right. Turn right at the road junction, then turn left. Continue to the far corner between the houses to enter the woodland.

❷ Follow the route to the right as you pass through the woodland gate. At the steps keep left and follow the sign to Glasslaw gate. Bear left here. You are

going to take the route to the right, but first stop to look at Shell House (decorated inside with shells). Follow the track to the right until you come to the road. Cross here and follow the woodland path. At the first Y-junction bear left. Cross the bridge then turn right. Continue past this bridge until you reach a similar one further on.

❸ From the next bridge you can view the stone structure of Lady Kennedy's bath. After a short incline turn left and follow the main track to the Glasslaw car park. At the exit keep left. At the main road turn left. Continue to the junction where you turn right to follow a country lane.

❹ When you reach the main road at Mains of Dunnottar farm, turn right for a short distance, then left into Dunnottar Castle grounds, which leads to the right of the castle.

❺ On the skyline you will see Stonehaven's War Memorial. Turn left. Where the road narrows, look out for a narrow path leading to the right. Follow this steep path down towards the harbour.

❻ Continue along the waterfront. Take the road to the left and into a car park. Continue until you turn left at a boardwalk, which leads back to the town square. Cross the main road back to the car park in the square.

further information

From Dunnottar Castle, the route follows a cliff path back to Stonehaven. However, owing to coastal erosion this path may be closed for repairs. Instead, retrace your steps and follow the pavement back to Stonehaven.

access information

Stonehaven, 25 km south of Aberdeen, is served by frequent rail and bus services. It can be reached from the south by the A90 or A92.

A scenic harbour view welcomes the walker at the end of this route.

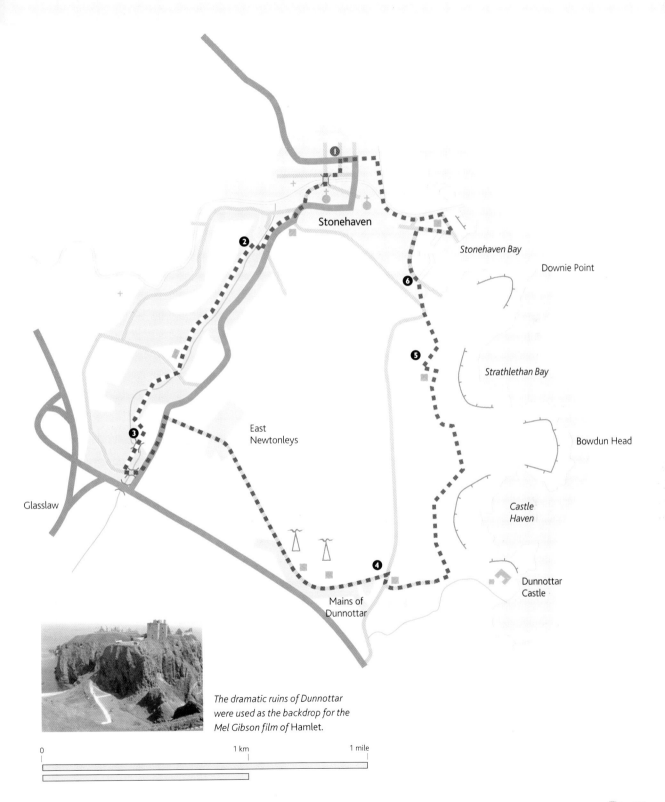

Stonehaven

Stonehaven Bay

Downie Point

East
Newtonleys

Strathlethan Bay

Bowdun Head

Glasslaw

Castle
Haven

Mains of
Dunnottar

Dunnottar
Castle

*The dramatic ruins of Dunnottar
were used as the backdrop for the
Mel Gibson film of* Hamlet.

0   1 km   1 mile

▲ Map: Landranger 38
▲ Distance: 12 km/7½ miles
▲ Walk ID: 1536 Ian Cordiner

Difficulty rating

Time

▲ River, Sea, Toilets, Wildlife, Birds, Flowers, Great Views, Food Shop

Collieston from Forvie Sands

This is a coastal walk of great variety. It starts at the estuary of the River Ythan and passes over sand dunes to the seashore. It then follows a coastal cliff path to the old fishing village of Collieston. The return route is more inland over old sand dunes.

❶ On leaving the car park turn right and go along the track. Continue straight on, keeping the River Ythan to your right.

❷ The path gives way to sand dunes. Follow the boundary markers until you reach the sea, where you turn left.

❸ Continue along the sandy shore for about a kilometre. Look out for the grey hut on the left. Cross the stream and head up the sandy track ahead. The main path goes left, but you should turn right here. When you reach the ruins of Forvie Church, follow the path to the right. Bear right at the fork. Go through the gate and turn right.

❹ The walk turns left but it is worthwhile taking the route straight ahead down into the old fishing village of Collieston. Continuing onwards takes you past the village shop to the harbour. Return to the walk by retracing your steps and rejoining the path.

❺ Take the track to the right. Follow a grassy path to the left. Pass through the gate and follow the marked route to the right. The indicated route is to your left but you take the less well-worn track to the right at the marker post.

❻ The path here is rather indistinct. Look out for a large sand dune then turn left. It does not really matter if you miss it, as you will eventually reach the main track again if you head straight on. Turn right at the larger track and follow it out of the nature reserve. Turn right and head back to the car park.

This walk is particularly attractive for the variety of landscapes and colours that you will see.

This walk takes you over sand dunes to the seashore at Forvie Ness.

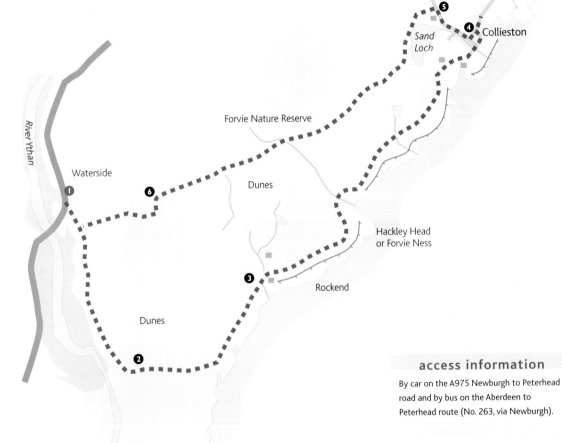

access information

By car on the A975 Newburgh to Peterhead road and by bus on the Aberdeen to Peterhead route (No. 263, via Newburgh).

further information

The sand dunes are rich in bird life. Parts of the sand dunes have restricted access, especially during the breeding season.

▲ Map: Explorer 425
▲ Distance: 11 km/6¾ miles
▲ Walk ID: 904 C. & J. Simpson

Difficulty rating

Time

▲ Sea, Pub, Toilets, Wildlife, Birds, Great Views, Food Shop, Mostly Flat, Public Transport, Ancient Monument

Sandend from Portsoy

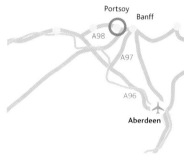

This simple walk follows the coast from the historic harbour at Portsoy to the lovely sandy beach and picturesque village at Sandend, returning by a inland route along paths through farmland.

❶ Follow the path away from the north west corner of Portsoy's picturesque medieval harbour. The path soon goes round to the left past a barn and up the hill above the gate. Keep following the path between the houses and the sea. Soon after you pass the last of the houses, the path goes round a barrier and joins a single track road. Ignore the turn to the right and follow the road.

❷ After a distance of 100 m turn right along the track. There is a small waymarker here. Keep following the track past a house until you reach a narrower path off to the right alongside a fence. Follow this for some way around the headland.

❸ Beyond the headland start heading inland again towards Sandend beach. The prettiest route drops down a narrow path and behind a ruin to reach the little bay. At the far end of the bay follow the path up over the grass and on towards the beach. You can join the return route to Portsoy from here but it is worth crossing the beach to the lovely village of Sandend first.

❹ After retracing your steps along the beach join the faint path which runs along the back of the beach and across this grassy area to reach a track. Once you join the track, follow it through a strange little gate and on past a house to reach a single track road. A couple of hundred metres along the road follow the turning left to North Arnbath.

❺ Where you see a building take the track off to the right at the bend. Continue along this track.

❻ Return to Portsoy along the outward route, which gives you good views of the village.

On the way back along the clifftops, you get a good view of the beautifully restored buildings nestling in the village of Portsoy.

Portsoy's main attraction is its
300-year-old harbour, which
was once a busy trading port
during the herring boom in the
19th century.

access information

Portsoy is on the main A98 trunk road
between Fochabers and Fraserburgh
and is well served by buses that ply the
coastal route between Elgin and Banff,
so access is easy. To reach the starting
point follow the signs to the harbour
from the A98. Sandend lies a short
distance from the main road but it is
still easy enough to reach it to get a
bus back to your starting point.

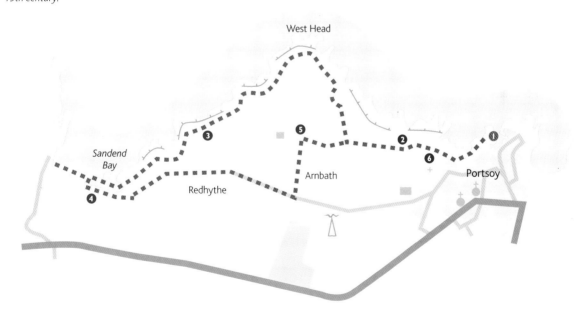

West Head

Sandend
Bay

Redhythe

Arnbath

Portsoy

0   1 km   1 mile

▲ Map: Explorer 382

▲ Distance: 10 km/6¼ miles

▲ Walk ID: 989 Alex Shepherd

Difficulty rating

Time

▲ River, Sea, Toilets, Museum, Wildlife, Great Views, Café, Food Shop, Nature Trail, Restaurant, Tea Shop

Montrose from Hillside

From Hillside, a good track follows the River North Esk upstream to the Morphie Dam and Salmon Ladder. Tracks and paths lead from here to the coastal sand dunes and back to Montrose.

❶ From the centre of Hillside, follow the curve up the hill on the A937 Marykirk–Laurencekirk road. Turn right at cottages before the end of the speed restriction and follow the road to the old Water Station. Cross the lade over the bridge at the Water Station. This track leads to the North Esk. Follow the track upstream – the Morphie Dam and Salmon Ladder will be in view. Return downstream.

❷ Take the grassy track which follows the river downstream to Kinnaber Bridge and the A92.

❸ Go over the bridge that crosses the lade. Follow the path downstream and under the road bridge until the lade meets the river. Having followed the path past two sets of cottages, cross a stile and continue seaward. The path crosses a small bridge and a small lagoon appears on the left. Take the track to the right or continue to the beach.

❹ At the salmon bothies take a diagonal track across to meet the main track. At the point where two plantations meet continue through a section of fencing opened to let walkers through.

❺ At the end of the plantation cross the left-hand then right-hand stiles on to a track along the old wartime airfield. Just past the wartime pill box go through a gate on to the golf course, which is common land, and continue past the Airfield Museum to Montrose.

❻ If you have taken the beach route or continued from the golf course and the Links of Montrose, you will reach the facilities at Montrose Beach.

Montrose is famous for its tidal basin, where the mudflats are a wintering site for migrant waders.

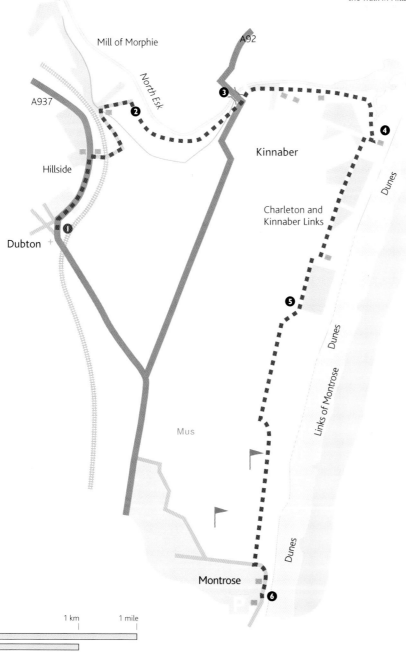

Mill of Morphie

A92

North Esk

A937

Kinnaber

Hillside

Charleton and Kinnaber Links

Dubton

Dunes

Mus

Links of Montrose

Dunes

Dunes

Montrose

0   1 km   1 mile

▲ Map: Explorer 416
▲ Distance: 5 km/3 miles
▲ Walk ID: 1437 D. B. Grant

Difficulty rating

Time

▲ Hills or Fells, Loch, Pub, Toilets,
Play Area, Wildlife, Birds, Flowers,
Great Views, Butterflies, Good for Kids,
Tea Shop, Woodland

Loch Ness.

Aldourie from Dores

A short circular walk at the northern end of Loch Ness which goes partly along the loch shore and partly along a ridge. You can see Loch Ness from one end to the other.

❶ Cross the B862 at the Dores Inn and go through the gate. Beyond the green shed there is a narrow path leading to the children's playpark. Follow this lochside path, passing many viewpoints. Continue to reach the entry to a wood.

❷ From the wood go down to the beach, where there is a good path, and follow it for 400 m, passing Tor Point, to a turn off on your right. This path goes to a higher level and follows the loch for a while before joining the main forestry track.

❸ On the main track go left, to arrive at the pier and anchorage. At the pier take the path leading off right. Follow this path uphill to a T-junction.

❹ Turn right and continue to a fork. At the fork go left. The track follows a fence for a while, to a viewpoint. Continue, to a grassy fork.

❺ Take the left fork here, downhill. Here you will find a good view to Dores.

❻ After about 200 m there is a mini-crossroads. Go left, downhill, and head back to the car park at Dores.

access information

Dores lies 13 km south west of Inverness, on the junction of the B862 and the B852. Park opposite the Dores Inn. If you wish to use public transport, there is a bus service from Inverness.

▲ Map: Explorer 416
▲ Distance: 4 km/2¹/₂ miles
▲ Walk ID: 794 D. B. Grant

Difficulty rating

Time

▲ River, Lake/Loch, Pub, Toilets, Birds, Flowers, Great Views, Public Transport, Nature Trail, Waterfall, Woodland

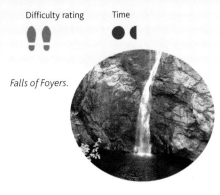

Falls of Foyers.

The Falls of Foyers

This is a short walk to enjoy at Foyers on the south shore of Loch Ness. Foyers is in two parts, Upper and Lower. The falls are best reached from Upper Foyers. The gorge descending into the Foyers River is narrow, wooded and very attractive.

❶ Start at the car park, next to the post office. Cross the road to the gate at the start of the walk.

❷ From the gate follow the signs 'Falls of Foyers', first to the Upper Viewpoint, then down to the Lower Viewpoint. From the Lower Viewpoint retrace your steps, passing the Upper Viewpoint, to a signposted junction.

❸ Take the path signposted 'To Path Network and Lower Foyers'. Keep to the main path, always going downhill. At a clump of rhododendrons there is another signpost.

❹ Take the 'Lower Foyers/Loch Ness' path (blue marker post). Stay on the main path; it eventually ends at a tarred road. If you go on to the lochside, return here. Retracing your steps you come to a wooden bridge over a pipeline.

❺ Cross the bridge and go left, up a few steps, to a junction. Turn left here for a few metres. Cross a wooden bridge and immediately turn right and retrace your steps to the car park.

further information

At Step 4, you can extend the walk by going on into Lower Foyers, on the lochside (this is one of the best areas for spotting the famous Loch Ness Monster!).

access information

Approach Foyers on the B852 from Inverness. Take the Upper Foyers road a kilometre and a half before Foyers. Park at the small car park next to the post office, on the main road. There is a limited bus service from Inverness to Foyers.

0   1 km   1 mile

▲ Map: Explorer 400
▲ Distance: 8 km/5 miles
▲ Walk ID: 1021 D. B. Grant

Difficulty rating

Time

▲ Hills or Fells, River, Pub, Toilets, Birds, Flowers, Great Views, Good for Wheelchairs, Butterflies, Gift Shop, Food Shop, Good for Kids, Tea Shop, Woodland

Kytra Lock from Fort Augustus

A good family walk. The towpath beside the Caledonian Canal is broad and firm all the way; there is no mud except at the riverside. There is a picnic area when you get to Kytra Lock.

❶ Start the walk from the car park at the Information Centre in Fort Augustus. Go along the A82, crossing the River Oich, to the canal. Stay on this side of the canal and go up to the top lock.

❷ At the top lock you join the canal towpath. You soon have the golf course on your left and the scenic River Oich on your right.

❸ After several kilometres the canal widens, making use of a pre-existing loch. Continue towards Kytra Lock.

❹ At Kytra Lock there is a picnic area. You return by the same path, as there is no complete path on the other bank of the canal.

access information

Fort Augustus is on the A82, south west of Inverness. Park in the main car park, which is in the centre of the village by the Information Centre.

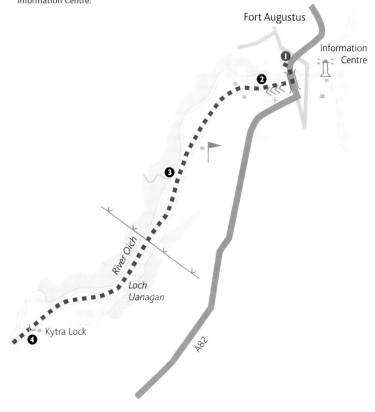

A beautiful view over the River Oich before it widens out is one of many fine vistas on this scenic stroll.

▲ Map: Landranger 12
▲ Distance: 9 km/5¹/₂ miles
▲ Walk ID: 1093 C. & J. Simpson

Difficulty rating

Time

▲ Sea, Castle, Birds, Great Views,
Mostly Flat, Public Transport

Noss Head from Staxigoe

A pleasant walk along a picturesque part of the coast immediately north of Wick, returning by a quiet inland road.

1 From the old harbour, follow the road northwards towards the farm at 'Field'. Pass through the farm and out to the coast. Continue northwards for about a kilometre.

2 You come to a more eroded part of the path approaching a bay called the Scholl. Keep following the path to the north end of the bay. After crossing a stile you will find the path cuts inland towards a gate in the wall.

3 Go over the gate and follow the path bearing left rather than going straight towards the lighthouse. The path reaches the road a hundred metres or so before the lighthouse. Turn left when you reach the road and follow it through the gate and back towards Staxigoe.

4 After turning the corner there is another long straight stretch of road. Turn left at the bend where the road is closed and follow another road leading towards Staxigoe.

5 When you reach the village carry straight on at the junction and follow the road back to reach your start point at the harbour.

A fine view of Sinclair Castle is the reward on offer for extending this walk slightly.

access information

From Wick follow the A99 north from the town centre and take the road signposted to Staxigoe. As you come into the village of Staxigoe there is a T-junction. Turn right here and follow the road round to the harbour where the walk starts. There are occasional buses here from Wick.

further information

From Step 3, the route can be extended with very little extra effort by following a road off to the right to visit Sinclair and Girnigoe Castles. Retrace your steps to continue the walk back to Staxigoe.

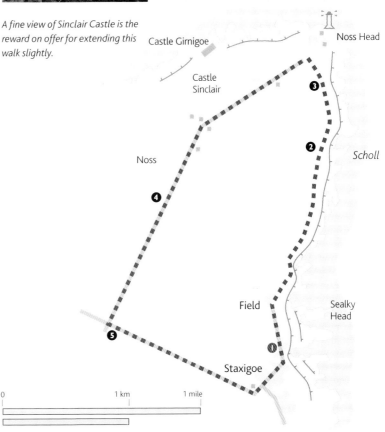

- Map: Explorer 433
- Distance: 6 km/3¾ miles
- Walk ID: 827 D. B. Grant

Difficulty rating

Time

- Hills or Fells, River, Sea, Pub, Stately Home, Wildlife, Birds, Flowers, Great Views, Butterflies, Food Shop, Good for Kids, Moor, Waterfall

Flowerdale Falls from Gairloch

This pleasant family walk goes from sea level at Gairloch to 150 m at the falls. The walk can be made shorter by returning the same way, but the alternative return route offers splendid views of hills and sea.

❶ From the car park take the gravel path leading upstream. It soon joins a road to Flowerdale House. After passing the house there is a T-junction.

❷ At the T-junction turn right. Go straight on to reach Flowerdale Mains (trekking centre). Here go through the gate and continue on this path to a three-way junction. Keep straight on, following the red posts, to reach the falls. At the falls cross the bridge and take the narrow path up the side of the falls. At the top go on for 200 m to another wooden bridge.

❸ Cross the bridge and follow the path downhill to a junction. If you want to go back to the car park quickly go right, and return by the outward route; to continue on this walk turn left, uphill, for a kilometre to a wooden bridge.

❹ Cross the bridge and follow the narrow but delightful path for a short way, well marked with blue posts. When you reach the lowest point on the path, cross the little burn at the blue post and go left for 20 m.

❺ Here you will see two blue markers on your right, marking a faint track going uphill to a viewpoint. You may either go up to the viewpoint or carry on along the lower path; the two paths soon meet again. Continue on this path to a T-junction with a main path.

❻ At the junction turn right and go through the double wooden gates. Shortly, you arrive at a DIY store. Pass it and immediately go right. You should now be at the Old Inn, by the car park.

access information

Charlestown (Gairloch) is on the A832. The car park is opposite the pier at the mouth of the river, conveniently by The Old Inn.

Gairloch is one of the most glorious and unspoilt wilderness regions in the whole of Britain.

further information

Flowerdale is a glen sheltered from most winds. It has a microclimate of its own, supporting plants such as bog orchids, bog asphodels, butterwort and sundew. Animals and birds such as voles, pine martens, stoats, weasels and buzzards can also be seen.

This bridge above Flowerdale Falls is as far as you go as you follow the footpath upstream.

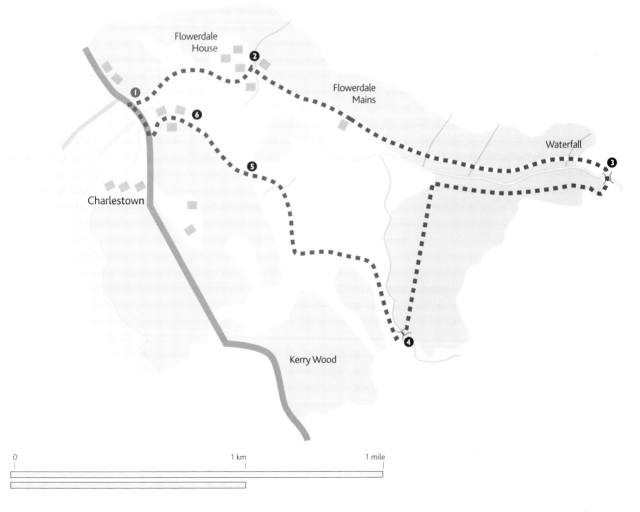

Flowerdale House

Flowerdale Mains

Waterfall

Charlestown

Kerry Wood

0   1 km   1 mile

▲ Map: Pathfinder 109
▲ Distance: 7 km/4¼ miles
▲ Walk ID: 1261 C. & J. Simpson

Difficulty rating
🥾🥾🥾

Time
●●●◗

▲ Sea, Birds, Great Views, Café, Moor, Tea Shop

Camas Mór from Rubha Reidh

A wonderful coastal walk from the lighthouse at Rubha Reidh to the sandy beach of Camas Mór. Although the distance is short, the route can be steep in places.

❶ The road drops quite steeply down to the lighthouse and round a hairpin bend to a parking area. The walk starts on the hairpin bend itself and goes through a 'gap' in the rocks. Follow the track until it starts to drop down towards a little jetty. Branch off right to cross the stream and head east, keeping parallel to the coast.

❷ Follow the traces of path along the cliff until around the point where you get a view of the sea stack, then head uphill, still more or less following the line of the coast.

❸ Keep following the coast and any path you can find to drop down to cross the stream before climbing back up the far side to reach the highest point of the route.

❹ Coming down you start to get good views of the beach at Camas Mór.

❺ To return to Rubha Reidh via the beach go down the long descending path. Go to the far (western) side where a rocky prow juts out towards the sea. Depending on the state of the tide you can go out round it on rocks and a boulder beach or through a little arch. On the other side is another bay.

❻ At the back of this bay are steep cliffs. A path winds up below the cliffs to join the grassier slopes beyond – there are a couple of fairly steep and narrow sections before you reach the main stream that you crossed on the outward route. Follow the stream easily uphill for 200 m or so and you pick up the path, which is followed back to the starting point.

access information

The starting point is reached by following the B8021 north west from Gairloch through Strath and Big Sand. The public road stops some way short of the lighthouse, but access is available to traffic visiting the lighthouse.

IMPORTANT: The route from steps 5 to 6 can only be followed when the tide is low.

From the top of the cliffs you get stunning views over the sandy bay at Camas Mór.

There's plenty of grand scenery to be enjoyed on this walk along the rocky headland of Rubha Reidh.

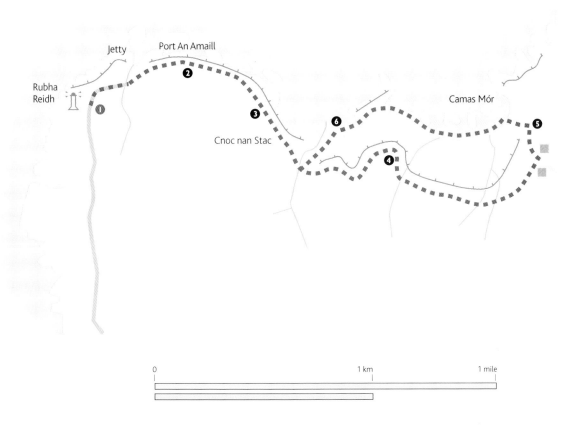

Difficulty rating

👣 👣 👣

Time

⬤ ⬤ ◖

Hills or Fells, River, Pub, Toilets, Stately Home, Wildlife, Great Views, Café, Gift Shop, Moor, Public Transport, Tea Shop, Woodland, Ancient Monument

Braid Hills

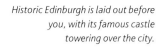

From the pretty Hermitage of Braid, the route climbs, encircles a golf course and heads up to the highest summit of the Braid Hills. It finishes with a short and pleasant road section through Morningside.

❶ From the top entrance to the Hermitage of Braid follow the road down past the Hermitage, keeping the stream on your left.

❷ The route then takes a large, well-defined path to the right. Follow this path down through woodland. The path crosses over the stream three times as it meanders, and the sides of the valley become increasingly steep. Cross under the low footbridge and continue along the path.

❸ You come to a clearing on the left and a prominent cliff-face known as the Agassiz Rock. Shortly afterwards there is an obvious path junction. Turn right on to the 'Howe Dean Path'. The path crosses over the stream and climbs steeply up through the dean to the edge of the field. Continue along the route by bearing left, and upwards, to a large road.

❹ Cross the busy main road, pass through the iron gate and turn left, to follow a path close to (but not on) the road. Continue, gradually descending, towards the golf course.

❺ At the entrance to the golf course, turn sharp right and follow the large red track. Follow the track around to the right and continue along it, gradually climbing up to the top of the Braid Hills and the summit, at 208 m.

❻ To descend, continue westwards, rejoining the red track. It quickly narrows into a path and becomes very steep. Take the left fork and continue down the hill until the path joins the main road. Turn sharp right and walk down the hill, beside the road. Continue straight ahead at a wide road junction. Continue along this road, passing by Morningside, back to the start.

Historic Edinburgh is laid out before you, with its famous castle towering over the city.

further information

Braid Hills is the name of one of Edinburgh's 'Seven Hills'. The other six can be seen on this walk. Directly north is Edinburgh Castle and the city centre, and directly south are the Pentland Hills.

access information

There is very limited parking on the road at the walk's starting point. Take care not to obstruct the entrance to the Hermitage. If there is no space, continue south uphill and park in the residential area or at the Braid Hills Hotel. Access by bus from the centre of Edinburgh is reasonably easy – catch any bus to Morningside, or No. 11, which passes the start of the walk.

Blackford Hill

Royal Observatory

Morningside

Hermitage of Braid

Visitor Centre ❷

❶

❸

❹

Braid Hills

❻

❺

Use the good information table on the summit of the Braid Hills to identify any landmarks you can see.

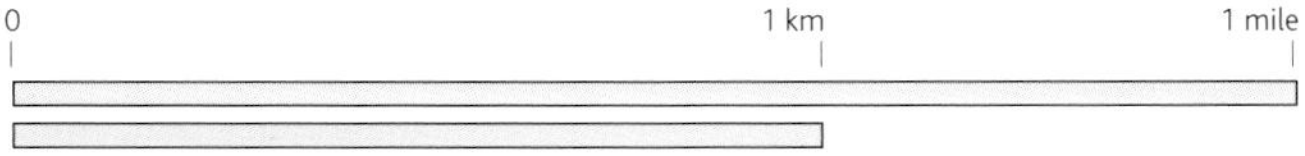

0   1 km   1 mile

▲ Map: Explorer 350
▲ Distance: 6 km/3¾ miles
▲ Walk ID: 110 Oliver O'Brien

Difficulty rating

Time

▲ Hills or Fells, Lake/Loch, Toilets, Church, Stately Home, Great Views

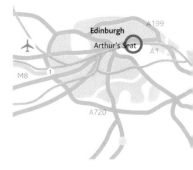

Arthur's Seat in Holyrood Park

A tour of the small but picturesque royal estate of Holyrood Park, in the heart of Edinburgh, climbing one of the city's Seven Hills – Arthur's Seat.

1 From the west (city centre) end of the car park, cross the road and climb a small flight of stairs. Turn right, and climb steeply on a good path with the crags (Salisbury Crags) on your left and dramatic views quickly opening up on your right. Follow the path to the end of the crags.

2 Before you get to the road, turn left and follow a smaller path, rising up slightly and over a brow. Take any of several paths down the broad, flat valley, going to the left of the water/marsh at the centre. Turn left and pass to the right of some small crags, then climb steeply but briefly uphill on a small path, aiming just to the right of the chapel remains.

3 Walk left to visit the chapel. Then turn back and follow a good path first back the way you came, walking straight ahead. Continue along the path into a smaller valley, parallel to the previous one. Follow the path up the right-hand side. The summit of Arthur's Seat is straight ahead. Continue up the path, climbing more steeply. The path peters out as it joins the main 'tourist' route up to Arthur's Seat. Turn right and follow it up.

4 On a fine day the views from the summit are magnificent. Turn back and head back down the tourist route, on a stepped path. Carry on straight down the tourist route, which becomes wide and grassy. Head down to Dunsapie Loch. Turn left and walk alongside the loch or follow a path around the left hand side of the small hill.

5 Meet the path beside the road. Carry on down beside the road, to the bottom.

6 Take a small path to the left just after the set of barrier gates on the road. Follow this path around the left hand side of the loch. Come back on to the road and walk back to the start.

Arthur's Seat is an extinct volcano in the heart of Edinburgh from where you have superb views of the city.

access information

The start of the walk is opposite the west end of the Palace of Holyroodhouse visitor car park. It is also a 10-minute walk from Edinburgh's central Waverley Station. From here, head out of the north east entrance and follow the road east to the Palace of Holyroodhouse, then south. By bus the start is a 10–15 minute walk from St Andrew's Square, Edinburgh's main bus station. Head south and climb to the High Street, then walk down the Royal Mile to the Palace of Holyroodhouse.

further information

Holyrood Park is a huge Royal Park open to the public. It is adjacent to the Palace of Holyroodhouse – Her Majesty the Queen's official residence in Scotland.

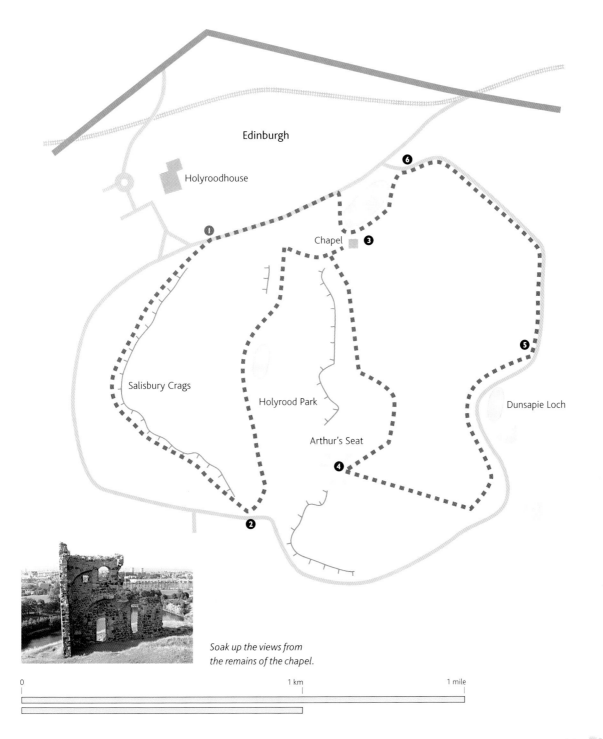

Edinburgh

Holyroodhouse

Chapel

Salisbury Crags

Holyrood Park

Arthur's Seat

Dunsapie Loch

*Soak up the views from
the remains of the chapel.*

0   1 km   1 mile

▲ Map: Explorer 344
▲ Distance: 11 km/6¾ miles
▲ Walk ID: 10 John Stewart

Difficulty rating

👣 👣 👣

Time

⬤ ⬤ ⬤ ◖

▲ Hills or Fells, Lake/Loch, Pub, Toilets, Great Views

The Pentland Hills

This walk lies in the heart of the peaceful Pentland Hills, just a few kilometres south of the hustle and bustle of Edinburgh.

❶ Take the path leading down the left-hand side of the Visitor Centre and follow it through the trees until it merges with the road.

❷ Continue along the road, skirting the reservoir and stream on the left. After passing a house with an adjacent white-posted gate, a second reservoir can be seen. At the far end of the second reservoir, make for a white house and cross the stream by the wooden bridge. Turn right on to a path in front of the house, entering a small field beyond.

❸ Walk towards the far left corner of the field and cross a stile adjacent to a wooden gate on to a well-defined track. Follow the steepish path upwards across several stiles, making for the saddle in the ridge just beyond. The path flattens out on to a broad ridge and soon crosses a well-defined ridgeway track.

❹ Turn left on to this track towards higher ground. Follow the track, which is fairly steep in parts, until you reach a large stone cairn surrounded by a stonefield. This is the highest point of the walk.

❺ Continue on the track running slowly downwards from the cairn until you reach a new ridgeway saddle. Cross the stile and continue on the path towards the top of the hill straight ahead, where there is a small stone cairn. From here, you can see most of the path leading all the way back down to the start of walk.

❻ Follow the path down from the cairn through grassy slopes. Carry on towards the start of the walk among the trees beyond. The track finally descends to the stream on the left. Cross the wooden bridge on to the road and turn right to reach the Visitor Centre and the car park.

On a clear day, you get marvellous views of the whole area from the top of the Pentland Hills – a chain of small, dome-shaped hills.

access information

The start of the walk is most easily reached by car. Take the main Edinburgh/Carlisle A702(T) road south out of the city to reach the Flotterstone Inn, which lies on the right side of the road about 5 km south of where the A702(T) crosses the Edinburgh by-pass (A720). Parking is available among the trees beyond the Inn and adjacent to the Visitor Centre.

Every August, Edinburgh Castle hosts a famous Military Tattoo within its walls.

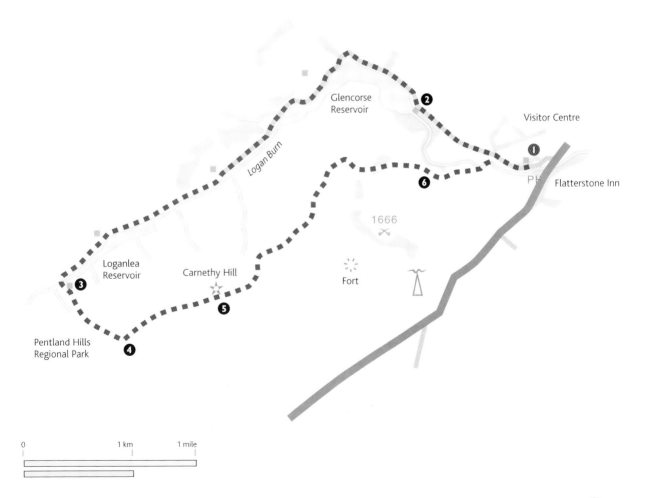

▲ Map: Explorer OL 32

▲ Distance: 11 km/6¾ miles

▲ Walk ID: 1463 Tony Brotherton

Difficulty rating

Time

▲ Hills or Fells, River, Toilets, Wildlife, Birds, Flowers, Great Views, Butterflies, Food Shop

Girvan

A714

Stranraer

A712

Newton Stewa

A75

Stroan Bridge Forest Trail

This route brings together various forest trails that start from the Visitor Centre at Stroan Bridge. It offers first-time visitors a sample of the superb upland scenery on offer without scaling the heights or plumbing the depths.

❶ Take the path signposted 'Forest Walks', which goes gently uphill. Cross a forest track to reach a multicolour-ringed directional post. Follow the path, which goes right, alongside a stone wall. Continue as far as the forest track.

❷ Follow the road left, eventually passing a yellow-ringed post, and arrive at a footbridge below Spout Head Waterfall. Continue along the path which runs pleasantly downhill to the road.

❸ Cross the road, going left, and take the access road off to the right for Caldons campsite. Cross the bridge over the Water of Trool and go right through the car park. Take the yellow trail off to the left, which is also part of the Southern Upland Way (denoted by a white thistle logo), soon to pass a signpost for Stroan Bridge.

❹ The route follows the Water of Trool downstream, with duckboards in places, to reach footbridges. To return directly to the start, cross the footbridge and follow the path to the left, soon to accompany the Water of Minnoch upstream to Stroan Bridge. To complete the full walk, continue past the footbridges to reach the confluence of the Water of Trool and the Water of Minnoch. The walk proceeds alongside the river bank to a stile and footbridge.

❺ Continue on the riverside path as far as the bridge. Cross the river and go straight ahead on the track to reach the road at the sign reading 'Holm'.

❻ Now turn right along the forest road leading back to Stroan Bridge and the start of the walk.

Spout Head Waterfall is one of the grander water features along your path through Galloway Forest Park.

access information

Turn off the A714 at Bargrennan, pass through Glentrool Village and then turn right (signposted 'Glen Trool'). Cross Stroan Bridge and park at the large car park near the Glen Trool Visitor Centre, where the walk starts.

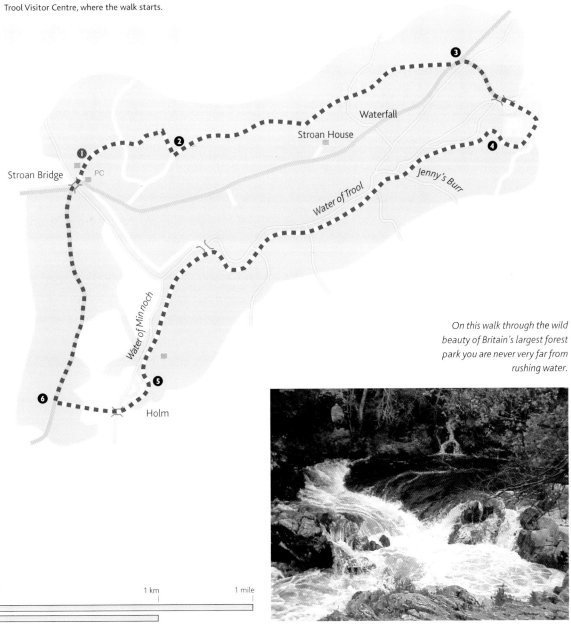

3

Waterfall

Stroan House

2

1

Stroan Bridge

PC

Water of Trool

Jenny's Burn

4

Water of Minnoch

5

6

Holm

On this walk through the wild beauty of Britain's largest forest park you are never very far from rushing water.

0		1 km	1 mile

▲ Map: Explorer 346
▲ Distance: 10 km/6¼ miles
▲ Walk ID: 121 Oliver O'Brien

Difficulty rating

Time

▲ Hills or Fells, River, Toilets, Church, Stately Home, Wildlife, Flowers, Great Views

Edin's Hall Broch from Abbey St Bathans

This scenic circular walk starts and finishes at Abbey St Bathans, an historic estate village. Along the route there is a medieval broch, two suspension bridges, profuse oak woodlands, and a moorland, all in a 10 km walk!

You cross Whiteadder Water a couple of times on spectacular suspension bridges.

❶ Follow the road south east through the village. Continue, bearing right and climbing. Take the small path that starts here to the left of the road and runs for a short way through woodland, before rejoining the road.

❷ The road turns sharp right. Take the path left dropping steeply to a stream. Cross the bridge and follow the path, gradually climbing. Turn left and go down beside a field. At the end of the field, turn right, and follow the path up, climbing steeply.

❸ Pass Edin's Hall Broch (the well preserved medieval fort) to its right, then bear left slightly to pick up a well-defined path going steeply down the hill, through a gate. After crossing a wall with stone steps turn sharp left. Turn right at the bottom of the field, staying on top of a ridge above the river's flat flood plain. Follow it round to the right. At a small junction bear left into a thicket.

❹ Cross the gate and follow the path to the left passing some cottages on your right. Cross the suspension bridge above Whiteadder Water. Follow the track on the other side, through open land and then through a forest, passing two signposts. Turn left on to a very quiet country road, and follow it uphill.

❺ At the junction turn left, cross over a stile and follow a track beside a field, crossing two gates and gradually dropping down into a valley. At a signpost join the Southern Upland Way. Turn left and follow the track. Cross the gate and continue on the track.

❻ At Whiteadder Water turn sharp right (signposted) and follow a small path with the river on your left. Turn left off the path and cross a large and very long suspension bridge and back to the start.

access information

From the north take the A1 to Cockburnspath, then follow unclassified roads south and uphill, signposted to Abbey St Bathans. From the south take the A1 to Grantshouse, turn off left (S) on to the A6112 for 10 km to Reston, turn right (W) on to the B6355 for 4 km, then right (N) on to an unclassified road signposted to Abbey St Bathans. There is no regular public service to Abbey St Bathans – the nearest access by bus is at Grantshouse on the A1 – 6 km north of the halfway point of this walk. Start by the village church, opposite a red phone box.

further information

Much of the walk is signposted
by small yellow arrows (for the
first part) or Long Distance Path
markers (for the last section).

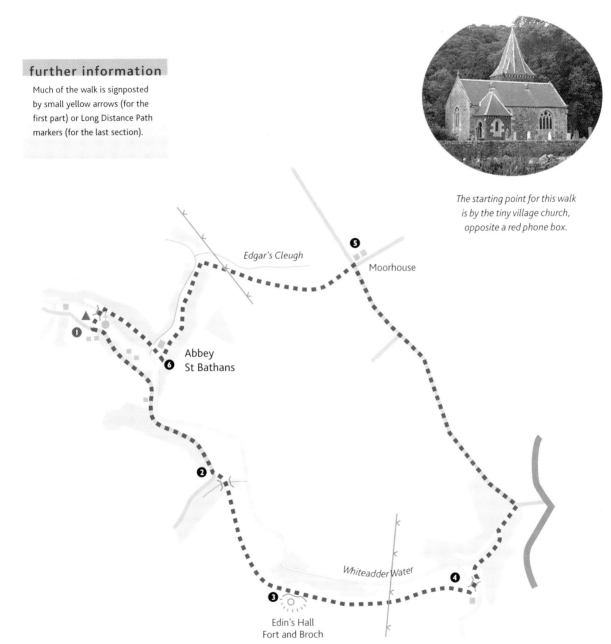

*The starting point for this walk
is by the tiny village church,
opposite a red phone box.*

Edgar's Cleugh

5 Moorhouse

Abbey
St Bathans

6

1

2

Whiteadder Water

4

3

Edin's Hall
Fort and Broch

0   1 km   1 mile

▲ Map: Explorer 326
▲ Distance: 4 km/2½ miles
▲ Walk ID: 902 J. & D. Howat

Difficulty rating

Time

▲ River, Pub, Toilets, Play Area, Church,
Wildlife, Birds, Flowers, Great Views,
Butterflies, Food Shop

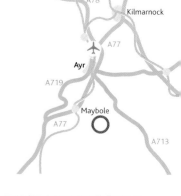

Lambdoughty Glen from Straiton

This walk goes along a country road followed by a picturesque scramble up one side of a fast-flowing burn and back on the other side, with wonderful views of waterfalls before returning to the picturesque village of Straiton.

❶ At the start of the walk follow the green arrows. Go straight on to the path at the end of the road and follow it until you reach the burn. Cross by the bridge. Turn to the left on to the road. The road goes uphill for about half a kilometre, passing Largs Farm.

❷ Turn to the left at the end of the trees to enter Lambdoughty Glen. A green arrow shows the way. The path to the left is easy to follow with steps cut in the earth, held in place by boards, and a bridge to cross the burn.

❸ At the bridge you recross the burn and see the largest fall of all (known as the Rossetti Linn because the painter Dante Gabriel Rossetti was thought to have contemplated suicide here). Continue on the high path, now fairly level.

❹ Turn right on to the road again as you leave the wood and walk back as far as the wooden bridge, to Straiton. Turn right at the T-junction. Continue past the church and back to the car park or parking place.

access information

From the A77 south of Ayr take the B7045 to Kirkmichael and on to Straiton. Park on the right or in the car park.

The grandest fall on your route is known as the Rossetti Linn, after the Pre-Raphaelite painter Dante Gabriel Rossetti, who is believed to have contemplated suicide at this point.

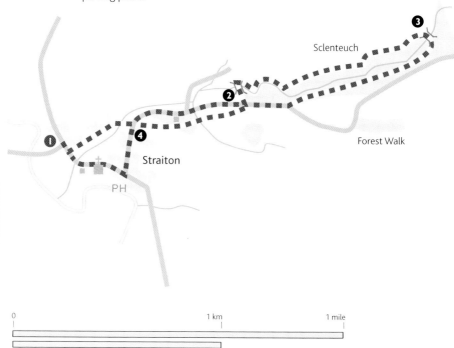

▲ Map: Explorer 326
▲ Distance: 5 km/3 miles
▲ Walk ID: 1201 Jude Howat

Difficulty rating

Time

▲ River, Wildlife, Birds, Flowers, Great Views, Butterflies

Wallace's Seat from Oswald's Bridge

The first part of this very pleasant walk follows the river through trees. At the turning point there is a seat by the river to enjoy the view (supposedly where William Wallace sat and contemplated his fight with the English).

❶ Turn left to cross the bridge over the river. Turn immediately left at the post with the green robin sign and descend the stairs to the river bank. The path is clear and takes you through some trees.

❷ A steep climb leads to the top of Three Knights Field to a viewpoint. At this point admire the view – on a clear day you can see as far as the Isle of Arran. Continue to follow the green robin waymarks.

❸ The green robin route crosses the stile here but this walk continues to the left, this time following red robin signposts which follow the path through Pheasant Nook Wood. Continue through Craighall Wood until high above the river where Wallace's seat can be seen.

❹ There are steps down to the seat to enjoy the view. When you leave the river, care should be taken to double back. The path continues along the river but as you walk away from the river you should see a narrow path which turns back in the direction you have come by. Stay close to the fence until you meet the obvious cart track on the left.

❺ Turn to the left out of the woods and walk along the broader cart track between fields and enjoy the pastoral views over Louden Law.

❻ Climb over the stile, turn right and you are back to the start. If you wish you can enter Leglen Wood opposite and visit the monument to William Wallace.

River Ayr.

access information

Leave the A77 at the Heathfield roundabout, on the Ayr bypass, to take the B743 towards Auchencruive. After a kilometre take the minor road to the right labelled SAC Auchencruive, Leglen Wood. Just before Oswald's Bridge take the road to the left and park. If this car park is busy there is further parking closer to Oswald Hall.

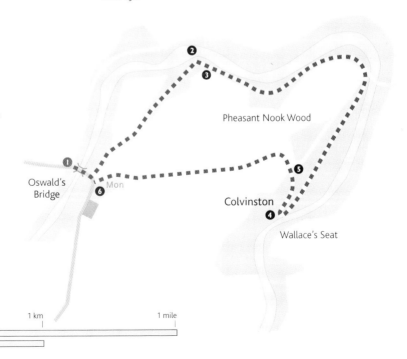

0   1 km   1 mile

▲ Map: Explorer 407

▲ Distance: 9 km/5½ miles

▲ Walk ID: 1067 C. & J. Simpson

Difficulty rating

👞👞👞👞

Time

●●●●◖

▲ Hills or Fells, Mountains, Sea, Great Views, Moor

Macleod's Tables from Osdale

This circular route is over the two hills, known as Macleod's Tables (North and South), which dominate the north west of Skye. The isolated location of the hills means they have excellent views to the Outer Hebrides.

1 From the B884 Dunvegan to Glendale road follow the track through the gate towards the ruin at Osdale.

2 Pass by the ruin and start to head uphill behind it. To pick up a path of sorts, head uphill to the corner of the fence on your left and cross a little stream just beyond it. Continue uphill to a gorge and follow its right-hand side until you can cross it. Head up through a hollow to the more open slopes to the top of the hill.

3 The summit of Healabhal Mhor (Macleod's Table North) is towards the far side of the flat summit plateau and is marked by a cairn.

4 To continue to the south table, walk south for about 200 m, after which there is a fairly abrupt drop towards a flattish col and the ridge leading to Healabhal Bheag (south table). The descent is easier than it looks. Beyond the col is a more obvious ridge over the small top and onwards to the climb up the south table.

5 The summit of Healabhal Bheag is marked by a trig point and a cairn. Continue north east past the second cairn until you see a prominent ridge which is followed for a few hundred metres. This ends in a prominent steep nose so you should descend the easier slopes on your left as you continue to follow the line of the ridge.

6 After dropping off the side of the ridge you can pick your own line – heading for the Osdale River, which is followed downstream. The best return route is to keep fairly close to the river until it begins to meander quite widely and then take an obvious direct route back to the road.

Your reward for reaching the summit is the stunning view over Loch Dunvegan, but it is safer to be off the hills by sunset.

access information

The starting point is about 2 km along the
B884 road from Dunvegan, just beyond the
bridge over the Osdale River. There is plenty
of parking, particularly near the bridge.
Public transport is limited, although the walk
could easily be done from Dunvegan without
the need for a car.

further information

There is another cairn, where there are
better views, about 100 m north east of the
summit of Healabhal Bheag.

❶

Osdale

❷

❸

Healabhal Mhor
(Macleod's Table
North)

❹

Glen Osdale

Osdale River

*This is the sort of rugged
countryside you can expect to be
covering on this hill walk.*

Healabhal Bheag
(Macleod's Table South)

❻

❺

0		1 km	1 mile

▲ Map: Explorer 380

▲ Distance: 8 km/5 miles

▲ Walk ID: 1303 Mike Taylor

Difficulty rating

Time

▲ Hills or Fells, Lake/Loch, Wildlife, Birds, Flowers, Great Views, Moor, Woodland

Lundie Craigs from Tullybaccart

A low-level walk in the Sidlaw Hills to the north of Dundee. A couple of short steep climbs but superb views over the Angus Glens and River Tay.

1 Carefully cross the A923 and follow the farm track to Tullybaccart Farm. Do not take the track to the disused quarry. Keep left and follow the main track slightly downhill and round the bend.

2 Near the start of the forest, branch sharp right and follow the grassy slope up the side of the wood, passing some shacks on your left. Climb the wire fence at the top and turn left to continue skirting the wood on a grassy path. As you reach the end of the forest fence you will see Ardgarth Hill about half a kilometre to the north east. Continue over open moorland to the top of Ardgarth Hill.

3 Pause to enjoy the view over the Tay Estuary to the south east and the impressive Lundie Craigs over the valley to the north. Descend into the valley below the craigs. Bear right on a narrow grassy footpath below the craigs. As it curves left, pass below some power lines and through/over a farm gate then head towards a second set of power lines leading up to the craigs.

4 You will see Long Loch in the valley below and the stone tower on Kinpurnie Hill beyond. Leave the path here and follow the power lines up the hill, picking up a narrow grassy path that leads to the trig point on the craigs.

5 Continue ahead towards the transmitter mast at the corner of Drumsuldry Wood. Pass through a wooden gate and follow the path along the top of the cliffs. Climb over/under the fence to your right leading to the valley. Enter the forest and join a path down through the trees.

6 Continue through the woods then follow the path as it turns sharp left and descends through some low hanging trees to Ledcrieff Loch. Walk across the earthen dam. At the far end turn right and follow the track to join the outward route, then back to the car park.

access information

There is a small car park on the west side of the A923. It accommodates about 14 cars if drivers park considerately.

The River Tay flows peacefully through the valley below the stone tower on Kinpurnie Hill.

An additional short walk to Laird's Loch and
Northballo Hill can be accessed through the
gate at the south end of the car park.

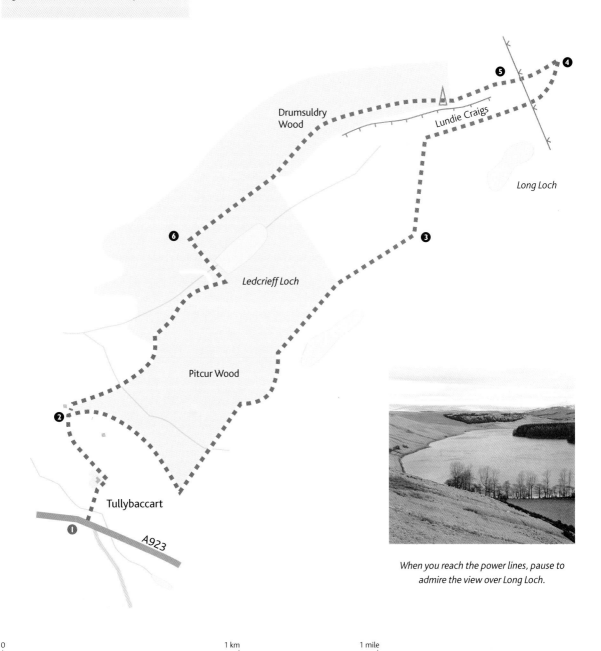

Drumsuldry
Wood

Lundie Craigs

Long Loch

5

4

6

Ledcrieff Loch

3

Pitcur Wood

2

Tullybaccart

1

A923

When you reach the power lines, pause to
admire the view over Long Loch.

0	1 km	1 mile

▲ Map: Explorer 406
▲ Distance: 11 km/6¾ miles
▲ Walk ID: 585 Ian Cordiner

Difficulty rating

Time

▲ River, Toilets, Great Views, Food Shop, Public Transport, Tea Shop

Peterculter from Aberdeen

A linear walk along the route of the old Deeside railway line, from Duthie Park to Peterculter (locally Culter). Although never very far from a main road, it is a very tranquil walk which also has some picturesque views over open countryside.

1 From the car park follow the sign, then turn left at the gap in the wall. Continue straight along the route of the old railway track.

2 A bridge has been removed, so you have to go down some steps and rejoin the route at the other side of a street. Where the same problem occurs further on, turn right at the steps, cross the busy main road, and rejoin the old railway route by climbing the steps. Continue along this path, which is well provided with seats to allow you to stop and admire the views.

3 Where yet another bridge has been removed, keep to the path which rises to the right. Admire the views to the south over a golf course. After passing the old platform, there are steps just beyond the next bridge. These will allow you to exit the walk here, should you wish. Turning right leads north to the A93 where it would be possible to catch a bus back into Aberdeen.

4 Continue across the main road. (Alternatively, turning right again takes you to the A93, which is about 200 m away, but doing so means you will miss some of the best views on the walk.) By now the walk passes much closer to the river.

5 You have now reached the platform for the old Culter station. Keep on until the track ends. Turn right up Howie's Lane. Continue up to the main A93 road.

6 At the top, turn left and cross the road to the bus stop where you can catch a bus back to the centre of Aberdeen.

Amazingly, it is possible to navigate a fairly peaceful, rural route through the granite city of Aberdeen.

further information

For those who enjoy railway history, it may be interesting to look out for old railway property and platforms. At one time, trains stopped at Holborn Street, Ruthrieston, Pitfodels, Cults, West Cults, Bieldside, Murtle, Milltimber and Culter.

access information

The walk starts at the car park at the
Polmuir Road entrance of Duthie Park in
Aberdeen. It can be reached by car or city
bus No.17 To return to Aberdeen it is a short
walk from the old railway route to the A93,
which is served by a regular bus services
(Nos.19, 24 and 201).

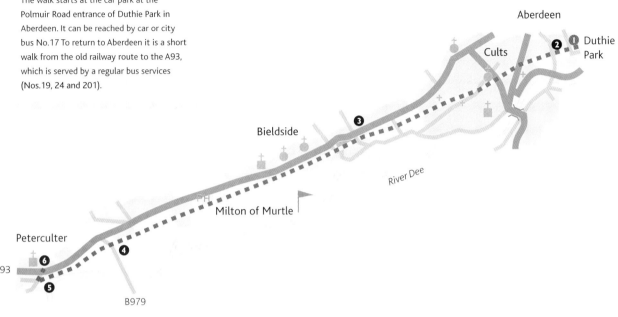

Aberdeen

Cults

Duthie Park

Bieldside

River Dee

Milton of Murtle

Peterculter

A93

B979

0   1 km   1 mile

▲ Map: Explorer 403
▲ Distance: 6 km/3¾ miles
▲ Walk ID: 1380 Ailsa Campbell

Difficulty rating

Time

▲ Church, Castle, Wildlife, Birds, Flowers, Great Views, Butterflies, Woodland

Abernethy Forest

This walk takes you through woodland, farmland and near a former mill with its waterwheel and lade still intact. There are views and a spectacular castle.

1 Pass through the gate and follow the track. Cross the tiny bridge over the burn. Turn left at the pylons. Turn left at the road and walk parallel to it. Pass through the gate and cross the car park. Pass through another gate and follow the track.

2 Turn left at the waymarked post. At the fork in the track carry straight onwards. The path leads off to the right. Follow the pink arrows to a stile. At the stile cross the road. Follow the track leading to the left. As the track meets the driveway leading to Aultmore House, turn right.

3 Follow the trail leading downhill and to the left. Cross the footbridge over the burn and follow the path along the side of a field. Follow the path round to Milton Croft (the site of the former mill). Pass through the gate and carry on down the made-up road towards the church. Turn right and follow the path between the field and the road, near Castle Roy.

4 Pass through the gate and along the side of the forest. Continue up the Forest Road. At the top there is a T-Junction. Take the road to the right then take a smaller track leading off to the right, downhill through the trees. At the bottom of the track pass through the gate and cross the duck boards. Follow the track around the edge of the field. Pass through the gate.

5 Turn left and return towards the burn. When the track meets the road turn right and walk down the road. Pass through the gate on your left and continue through the woods.

6 Take the first track leading to the left and walk behind the school grounds. Cross over the stream and follow the track. Pass through the gate. Follow the pavement along the side of the road until you return to the starting point.

A hike through the Abernethy Forest, one of Britain's least-altered habitats, gives you a taste of what the Highlands were like 300 years ago.

Craigmore Wood

Castle Roy

④

Milton

⑤

③ Aultmore

⑥

Sch

Alt Mor

Nethy Bridge ①

②

access information

The village of Nethy Bridge is to be found east of the A95, about 15 km north east of Aviemore in the Abernethy Forest. The start is found on the road south of the school.

0	1 km	1 mile

▲ Map: Explorer 419, 418
▲ Distance: 8 km/5 miles
▲ Walk ID: 839 D. B. Grant

Difficulty rating

Time

▲ Pub, Wildlife, Birds, Flowers, Great
Views, Butterflies, Gift Shop, Food
Shop, Good for Kids, Public Transport,
Tea Shop, Woodland

Anagach Wood, Grantown-on-Spey

This is a popular walk with visitors to Grantown. Accessible from the town centre, the walk winds through pine woods, first following a military road then through glaciated scenery with old glacial lakes.

1 Take the broad path (the Old Military Road indicated by a red arrow). Go through an iron gate. A few metres on there is a junction. Go left to the end of the old military road, ignoring all other paths.

2 Turn off left on a narrow path and you immediately come to a fork. Go right at the red marker post and walk along the crest of a ridge to reach a fork. Keep left and you reach a junction after 20 m. The route goes right, to reach a crossroads after 50 m.

3 At the crossroads go left through a birch wood to arrive at an open glade. A few metres into the glade go right on the broad path crossing it. Carry on to a fork near Craigroy Farm.

4 At this fork turn left onto a gravelly track. When you arrive at another fork go left to a crossroads. Turn right at this crossroads. (Watch this one; it looks as though you should go straight on.) Keep on to reach a T-junction at a wire fence and burn.

5 Turn left on to the Speyside Way. Follow it to a fork. At this fork go left, to reach another T-junction. Turn right and go on to another T-junction. Turn right at the T-junction to arrive at the edge of the golf course.

6 At the golf course go left at the red/blue post on a narrow track, passing old glacial lakes to the left and right. When you come to an open glade take the right fork (red post) and cross the glade to the next red marker post straight ahead of you. From the second marker post you join a broad path. Pass the Curling Rink to a metal gate, where you join a wide track. When you join the wide track go straight on for 100 m to reach the car park.

access information

From the town square in Grantown go down Forest Road. The car park is at the road end. Public buses operate between Inverness, Aviemore and Grantown.

The heart of the Highlands, Grantown-on-Spey is a purple haze when the heather is in bloom in August.

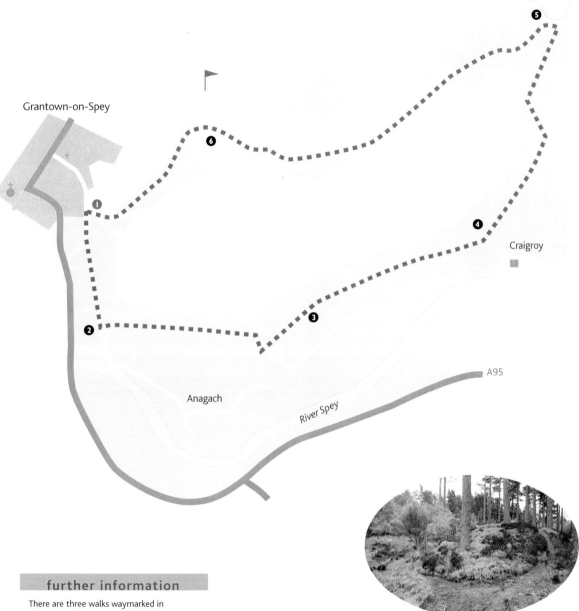

Grantown-on-Spey

❺

❻

❹

Craigroy

❸

❷

A95

Anagach

River Spey

further information

There are three walks waymarked in
Anagach Wood, all starting from the same
car park. This is the Red route and is the
longest walk.

*Paths get progressively narrower
as they fork through trees
and heather.*

0   1 km   1 mile

▲ Map: Explorer 406

▲ Distance: 11 km/6¾ miles

▲ Walk ID: 398 Ian Cordiner

Difficulty rating

Time

▲ River, Toilets, Castle, National Trust/NTS, Great Views, Public Transport

Crathes Castle from Banchory

A gentle walk along a former railway line, at first parallel to the River Dee. It enters the ground of Crathes Castle and returns along a wooded route.

❶ Go to the east end of the car park. Enter Bellfield park and walk across the grass to the opposite corner. Cross the rough car track and follow the tarred footpath, the old railway route. Continue under the bridge and take the path to the right. Again keep right, following a route parallel to the cemetery.

❷ Turn right at the next main junction (parallel to the river). Again keep right. At the junction take the second road from the right (the first one goes down to the river). Continue past a fisherman's hut to a straight path which was once the old railway line. Continue straight on and bear right into the woods.

❸ At the stream turn sharp left and climb a few steps up to the old railway line route again, then turn right. Follow the old railway route. Turn right at the Milton of Crathes sign. Enter the car park and follow the white signs to the end of the car park. Cross the old mill lade and go straight on, following the signs to Crathes Castle.

❹ Follow the route through the castle grounds to the tree-lined road and out at the main entrance at Harestone Road.

❺ Continue straight on across the new Hirn/Echt road and bear right along a disused loop road until you reach the next road. Turn right. Soon you turn left through an obscured metal gate through the wooded pathway.

❻ Turn left and walk the short distance to the main road (A93). Turn right and walk towards the supermarket. Cross the A93. Walk away from the main road, past the main entrance to the supermarket. Turn right at the end of the buildings. Walk towards the south west corner of the building where you find a small path. Follow this path towards the river. Turn right and retrace your route back to the car park.

access information

Easily reached by car or bus along the A93. There is a frequent bus service, No. 201 from Aberdeen. The walk starts at Bellfield car park, Dee Street, Banchory.

The picture of tranquillity, the River Dee winds along a broad valley, flanked on either side by pine forests, wild heathery moors and high hills.

One of the best preserved castles in Scotland, Crathes Castle on Royal Deeside is a massive 16th-century fortress with fairy-tale turrets.

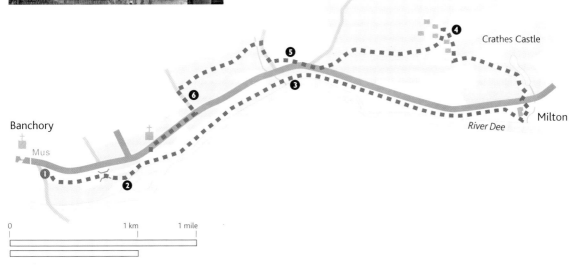

Crathes Castle

Banchory

Mus

River Dee

Milton

0   1 km   1 mile

further information

Crathes Castle dates from the 16th century, and has world-famous gardens with ancient yew hedges. Entry to the castle grounds and gardens is free all year round, but there is an entrance fee for the castle (open daily, April to October).

▲ Map: Explorer 395
▲ Distance: 8 km/5 miles
▲ Walk ID: 1069 Ian Cordiner

Difficulty rating

Time

Hills or Fells, Mountains, River, Lake/Loch, Toilets, Church, Wildlife, Birds, Great Views, Nature Trail, Woodland

Knockie Viewpoint from Glen Tanar

This walk passes through pastoral scenery before entering a section of forestry plantations. It continues close by a stream for a large part of the route. Once past a small fishing loch the path skirts the Water of Tanar.

❶ As you leave the car park cross the road to the bridge over the Tanar. Take the route to the right (if you wish to visit the Visitor Centre, go left). Follow this track away from the Visitor Centre and bear left.

❷ Just off the track is the tiny St Lesmo's Chapel, built in 1870 and it is still in use today. Go through the gates then turn right. Continue left up the rise. Continue straight on at the crossroads, into the forestry plantation. Turn right where the path forks.

❸ Admire the view from the Knockie Viewpoint, before continuing down the hill where you take a left turn. Along this stretch there are some restful views along the waterside.

❹ When you reach the bridge, turn right and cross it. Continue straight on. After crossing the bridge with the low walls, turn right.

❺ Ignore the road from the left and bear right here. To the left of the path there is a small attractive fishing loch. Turn right at the next junction and continue to reach a bridge with rails. Cross the bridge and turn left.

❻ Look out for a marker post here. Take the grassy path to the left and follow it along the riverside until you return to the previous track. There are some other grass paths and sheep tracks, but keeping to the left allows you to keep by the waterside. Retrace your route to the visitor centre and back across the bridge to the car park.

Part of the walk takes you through damp pine forest where the floor is lined with moss and ferns.

access information

Several kilometres west of Aboyne, on the South Deeside road B976, take the unclassified road west to Glen Tanar until you reach the car park for the Braeloine Visitor Centre.

further information

Many fine specimens of Scot's pine are found growing naturally through a carpet of heather and bracken. These trees are rare remnants of the old Caledonian pine forest which once covered the whole area.

Majestic Scot's pine line the banks of the Water of Tanar flowing down the glen.

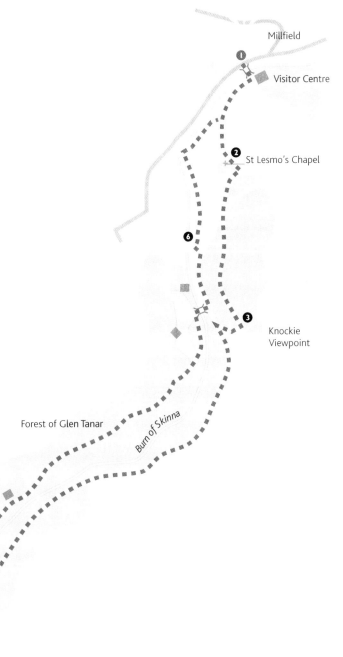

Millfield

Visitor Centre

St Lesmo's Chapel

Knockie Viewpoint

Forest of Glen Tanar

Burn of Skinna

Glen Tanar

0   1 km   1 mile

▲ Map: Explorer 429

▲ Distance: 14 km/8³/₄ miles

▲ Walk ID: 1037 A. Higginbottom

Difficulty rating

👣 👣 👣

Time

⬤ ⬤ ⬤ ⬤ ◖

▲ Mountains, Lake/Loch, Wildlife, Birds, Flowers, Great Views, Butterflies, Moor, Public Transport, Woodland

Coire Lair from Achnashellach

This fine walk goes up through the forest and over the Coulin Pass into the Glen. It then follows the base of Beinn Liath Mhor to the entrance to Corie Lair, before descending back through the forest to the start of the walk.

❶ Take the track by the phone box next to the car park in Achnashellach and head towards the railway station. Go across the railway line and up the forestry track bearing slightly right and through the gate..

❷ Go across at the forestry track crossroads and up the track signposted Coulin Road. Keep on going up the track, crossing over a bridge where there are good views to the right.

❸ Follow the track through the forest with occasional views of the mountains across the glen. Go through the gate in the deer fence and towards the bridge.

❹ After crossing the bridge turn left, continuing on a forestry track. Follow this until you reach the hut or small bothy known as the 'Teahouse' or 'Teashack'. Continue over the bridge and follow the stalkers' track up the Glen.

❺ Where the path joins the path from Corie Lair, turn left and start to follow the path downhill. Continue on down through the forest until you come to a gate in the fence.

❻ Go through the gate and join a forestry track where you turn right. Follow the track on down through another gate and turn sharp right at the crossroads, back over the railway line and on down to the start of the walk and the car park.

Beinn Liath Mhor in winter.

access information

The car park is situated on the A890 Achnashean/Lochcarron road by the phone box at Achnashellach. This is also where the railway station is found, making it easily accessible by train.

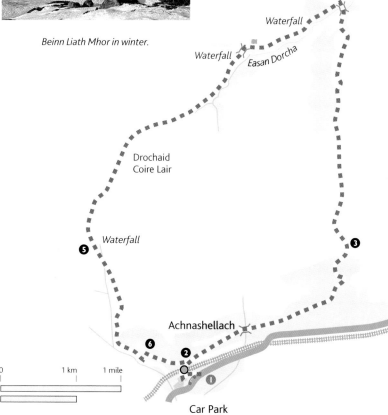

Waterfall

Waterfall   Easan Dorcha

Drochaid Coire Lair

Waterfall

❺

❹

❸

❻   ❷   ❶

Achnashellach

Car Park

0   1 km   1 mile

- ▲ Map: Pathfinder 144
- ▲ Distance: 6 km/3¾ miles
- ▲ Walk ID: 777 D. B. Grant

Difficulty rating

Time

▲ Hills or Fells, Wildlife, Birds, Great Views, Moor, Woodland, Ancient Monument

Fyrish Hill, Easter Ross

A pleasant walk in Easter Ross offering splendid views to the Cairngorms, Ben Wyvis, the Affric and Fannich ranges and the Cromarty Firth. The walk is between Evanton and Alness and climbs to 450 m. There is an unusual summit monument.

1 Take the path leading out of the car park. At the crossroads go straight on, soon crossing a wooden bridge over a gorge.

2 At the next crossroads go straight on to another set of crossroads (near a large pond to your left).

3 From this crossroads keep straight on, across open moor. The walk climbs steadily to the summit first through pine forest then across open moorland above the treeline.

4 Return to the car park from the summit by taking the path that starts a few metres from the monument and a few metres above your outward path. After about one kilometre you reach a junction.

5 At this junction go straight on and quite soon you come to the crossroads you crossed earlier.

6 Go left on to your outward path, back to the car park.

access information

From the A9, take the B9176 south-west of Alness. After 3 km take a left turn on to an unclassified road signposted Boath. After a further 2.5 km you reach the small car park, on your left.

The monument at the summit.

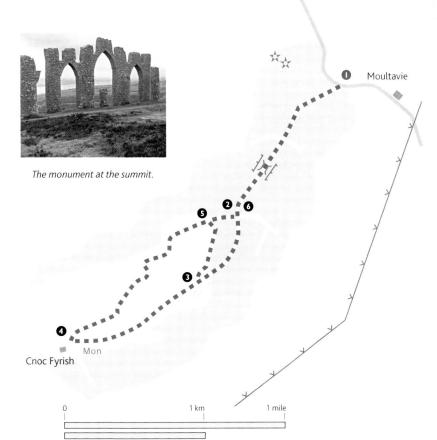

further information

The large, unusual monument at the summit was built in 1783 by Sir Hector Munro of Novar, who once commanded British Forces in India. When he returned home he provided work for destitute local people following the Highland Clearances.

Index

acknowledgements

The publishers wish to thank the
following for the use of pictures
TONY BROTHERTON: p.9, 43
COLLECTIONS :p.8 Dennis Barnes
CORBIS: p.11 Ric Ergenbright,
18 Roger Tidman, 22 Peter Hulme/
Ecoscene, 26 Niall Benvie 32 Ric
Ergenbright, 36 Adam Wolfitt, 42
Niall Benvie, 50 Adam Wolfitt,
52/3 Jason Hawkes, 54 Niall Benvie,
56 Macduff Everton, 58/9 Steve
Austin/Papillio
IAN CORDINER: p.21, 23, 60, 61
**HUTCHISON PICTURE
LIBRARY:** p.312
GETTY IMAGES: p.10 Graeme
Norways/Stone, 38 Chris Close/
The Image Bank, 40 David
Paterson/Stone
DAN GRANT: p.29, 30, 33, 57
JUDE HOWAT: p.12, 13, 14, 46, 47
OLIVER O'BRIEN: p.16, 17, 44, 45
COLIN AND JOANNE SIMPSON:
p.15, 24, 25, 34, 35, 48, 49, 62
MIKE TAYLOR: p.51